Nourishing Seeds of Faith

Nourishing Seeds of Faith

26 CHILDREN'S SERMONS

~

Virginia H. Loewen

RESOURCE *Publications* · Eugene, Oregon

NOURISHING SEEDS OF FAITH
26 Children's Sermons

Resource Publications
An Imprint of Wipf and Stock Publishers
199 W. 8th Ave., Suite 3
Eugene, OR 97401

www.wipfandstock.com

PAPERBACK ISBN: 978-1-4982-9228-3
HARDCOVER ISBN: 978-1-4982-9230-6
EBOOK ISBN: 978-1-4982-9229-0

Manufactured in the U.S.A.   06/24/16

To God's children, both young and old, with a prayer that your
faith will be nourished by God's word

Contents

Preface

Since the publication of *Planting Seeds of Faith* and *Growing Seeds of Faith*, I have continued to teach children about God and how God wants us to live. *Nourishing Seeds of Faith* is my third collection of nondenominational messages intended to educate and to provide spiritual food for youngsters. Beginning with Advent, the mini-sermons follow the birth, life, death and resurrection of Jesus. Interspersed throughout the book are messages appropriate for seasonal and secular holidays such as Father's Day, a patriotic celebration, and Thanksgiving.

Writers For Kids and the Christian Writers Roundtable in State College, Pennsylvania, have provided support and encouragement in this project. Their critiques have included comments such as "Wonderful teaching," "A great lesson brought to a child's level," and "I love these mini-sermons. I wish our church did them!"

As the apostle Paul advised young Timothy, "Tell these things to the brothers. This will show that you are a good servant of Christ Jesus. You will show that you are made strong by the words of faith and good teaching that you have been following. People tell silly stories that do not agree with God's truth. Do not follow what these stories teach. But teach yourself only to serve God." —I Timothy 4:6,7 (International Children's Bible)

This is my task for the children and for myself. I pray that it is yours, too.

∼

Introduction

"Let the little children come to me. Don't stop them. The kingdom of heaven belongs to people who are like these little children." —Mark 10:14b (International Children's Bible)

Children are a vital factor in the growth formula of the Christian Church. But attracting four- to eight-year-olds, holding their attention, and teaching them about God can be a daunting task. *Nourishing Seeds of Faith* is a nondenominational resource to aid pastors and laity who teach children in family worship services. Each lesson is based on a passage of scripture and offers ideas for applying it and sharing faith away from the church. (Note: Use the Index to find topics of interest.)

I pray that the following guidelines and tips will help to nourish the seeds of faith that have been planted so that they will grow into a bountiful harvest.

Guidelines and Tips for *Nourishing Seeds of Faith*

* Begin your preparations with prayer for guidance that you may speak so that the children will listen and learn about God's love for them.

* Carry props in a bag, basket, box, bucket, or any container appropriate for the topic or the season.

* Gather the children around you at the front of the sanctuary so that they face you, and you face the congregation. (If the children face the congregation, it can become a "show" for the children.) Sit at their level.

* Tell—don't read—the message. Jot notes on a large index card, or copy the lesson pages and keep them on your lap as you talk.

* Read pertinent verses of scripture directly from a Bible.

* Use language the children understand. Adapt the sermons to the ages of the children, their attention spans, and their experiences. Get to the main point quickly and focus on it. Allow five to ten minutes per message.

* Use a lapel or portable microphone. Repeat children's questions and answers clearly for the congregation's appreciation. Pause for children to respond to questions and ideas.

* Expect logical answers from children, but remember, also, to expect the unexpected. Be prepared for a few laughs—good medicine for the soul. Parentheses ( ) indicate some possible answers. Assure the children when they give good answers.

* Make it fun and interesting. Be loving, but firm, if children become too noisy or excited.

* Add or substitute your own appropriate experiences or anecdotes. Asterisks (*) mark some opportunities to do this.

* In children ages four through eight, understanding occurs at different levels. Include "Stretching Further" if more perceptive children need to be challenged. Use it as part of the basic lesson or in discussion that continues in a Sunday School class or midweek program.

* At the end of the sermon, restate the lesson learned (what the children should remember) and ask them to say it with you.

* Prayer: Ask the children to bow their heads and, if time allows, repeat phrases after you.

~

Show that you are made strong by the words of faith and good teaching that you have been following.—I Timothy 4:6b (International Children's Bible)

~

A House of Bread

Theme: Jesus satisfies our deepest longings.

Scripture: Jesus said, "I am the bread of life." —John 6:35a

Preparation: Bring a gingerbread house or photos of a variety of houses, which can be found online by searching *gingerbread houses photos*.

Are you getting ready to celebrate Christmas? Are you putting up decorations? Maybe you will have a Christmas tree. I've noticed that some folks make gingerbread houses at this time of year. Have any of you helped to make a gingerbread house?

I brought some pictures of gingerbread houses to show you. There are small ones, big ones and very large, fancy houses in these photographs.

Have you ever wondered why gingerbread houses are made especially at Christmastime? What does gingerbread have to do with Christmas? Was Jesus born in a gingerbread house?

What kind of place was Jesus born in? Jesus was born in a place where animals were kept. It may have been a cave. It certainly was not a gingerbread house.

I learned that gingerbread was first made more than 1,000 years ago in Europe—in Germany, France and England. Ginger cakes were baked for celebrations and holidays. Sweet, baked treats were made with ginger because the spice helped them stay fresh and last longer. At that time plastic wrap and plastic bags had not been invented.

Then about 200 years ago, the Grimm Brothers wrote a story about Hansel and Gretel. Do you know that fairy tale? Hansel and Gretel were lost in the woods when they came upon a house made of bread with a roof of cake. After that story was written, German bakeries made decorated gingerbread houses with icing for snow on the roofs.

When people moved to America, they brought the idea of gingerbread houses with them. Making gingerbread houses is now part of the Christmas season celebration for many families.

So, do you think there is any connection between ginger-**bread** houses and Jesus? I think we can make a connection. What is the name of the town where Jesus was born? Do you know that the name *Bethlehem* means "house of bread"?

Is there bread in any of the stories you know about Jesus? Jesus fed more than 5,000 people with five loaves of bread and had twelve basketfuls left over (John 6:1–13). Jesus taught his disciples to pray to God, "Give us this day our daily bread" (Matthew 6:11). At the Last Supper that Jesus shared with his disciples, he called the bread "my body" (I Corinthians 11:24). And Jesus said, "I am the bread of life. Whoever comes to me will never be hungry, and whoever believes in me will never be thirsty" (John 6:35).

Does this mean that if we believe in Jesus, we will never have to eat or drink again? No. We need to eat and drink to keep our bodies alive. There's another kind of food that we need. We are hungry for spiritual food. Jesus satisfies our hunger for love and for hope. He tells us that we can be forgiven when we have done something wrong. If we believe in him, we can live with him in his house in heaven forever. In this way Jesus is the bread of life.

Stretching Further:

With adult volunteers, have the children make gingerbread houses to display in their classrooms or in an area where adults can also enjoy them. You may want to serve gingersnaps for a snack.

Let's pray.

Our Father, we thank you that we can celebrate Christmas and build gingerbread houses. Thank you for the food we eat. And thank you for Jesus, the bread of life. We invite him into our hearts. Help us to love you and to love one another. In Jesus' name. Amen.

∼

Christmas Mail

Theme: The reason for our joy is Jesus.

Scripture: But the angel said to them, "Do not be afraid; for see—I am bringing you good news of great joy for all the people: to you is born this day in the city of David a Savior, who is Messiah, the Lord." — Luke 2:10,11

Preparation: In a small, seasonally-decorated basket or box, place a varied assortment of Christmas cards, used or new, so that each child may hold one. Also bring blank postal cards, one per child.

It will soon be Christmas Day. Do you get excited when you think about Christmas coming? Tell me some things that happen during the weeks before Christmas.

I've been getting a lot of mail. I brought some of it to show you. (*Hand a Christmas card to each child.*) What do we call this kind of mail?

Tell me what you see on your Christmas card. (*birds and other animals, snowmen, children, candles, toys, bells, snow scenes, candy canes, Christmas trees, Santa Claus or Father Christmas, angels, a star, camels, the Magi, Jesus in a manger, Mary and Joseph, etc.*)

Why do people send Christmas cards? (*because it's a special time of year, to keep in touch with family and friends, especially those who live far away, etc.*) What do Christmas cards often say? What are some words we find on Christmas cards? (*Merry Christmas and Happy New Year; best wishes for happiness, joy, peace, blessings, etc.*) One card says, "What better time than Christmas for wishing joy and cheer to all the special people who touch our lives each year. Have a Merry Christmas and a Happy New Year."

Another kind of card came in the mail for me the other day, along with a package. My daughter sent me a birthday card and a present because my birthday is in the week before Christmas.* That made me think about the real reason we celebrate Christmas. Whose birthday do we celebrate on Christmas Day?

Then I thought, *We are Christians. We believe that God sent Jesus to show us what God is like. Shouldn't the Christmas cards that Christians send say something about Jesus Christ?*

I wondered, too, how the custom of sending cards at Christmastime got started. I learned that in London, England, in 1843, more than one hundred fifty years ago, a man named Henry Cole wanted to send letters to his friends at Christmastime. But he didn't have time to write and sign a letter to each of his friends. So he asked an artist to draw a design that could be printed on a card about this size. (*Show postal card.*) It would have one message that he would send to everyone. In the middle of the card the artist showed a family eating Christmas dinner. The drawings on the sides of the card showed people giving clothes and food to those who needed them. Ivy, grapes and vine leaves decorated the edges. The message on the card said, "A Merry Christmas and a Happy New Year to You." That was the first Christmas card. Henry Cole had 1,000 cards like that printed, and he sold the ones that he didn't use.

People liked the idea of having cards printed with drawings on them at Christmastime. Artists added other things to the cards they drew: mistletoe, holly, mail-wagons in the snow, turkey, children, animals and fairies. Later on, they added Father Christmas, Saint Nicholas, Santa Claus and Christmas trees. Sometimes they showed the countryside in spring and summer with flowers, butterflies and birds. They wanted to remind people that nature was only taking a rest in winter and there would be warm, sunny days again.

In America a printer named Louis Prang decided to have art contests for people to draw Christmas card designs. The winners won money for their drawings. Many of the winning pieces showed scenes from the Bible, including the birth of Jesus. So it wasn't until about forty years after Henry Cole had his first Christmas card printed that some cards began to show manger scenes with Mary, Joseph and Jesus. That surprised me. I didn't know that, for so long a time, Christmas cards didn't say or show anything about Jesus.

What I learned was that the first Christmas card and most of the Christmas cards in more than one hundred fifty years have been sent for this reason only: to wish family and friends best wishes of the season and for the new year.

Among the best wishes I often see, however, on Christmas cards is the word "joy." Santa Claus, Christmas trees, Christmas cards and toys are fun, but let's remember the most important reason for being happy at Christmastime. Listen to what Luke tells us in the Bible: "But the angel said to them, 'Do not be afraid; for see—I am bringing you good news of great joy for all the people: to you is born this day in the city of David a Savior, who is the Messiah, the Lord'" (Luke 2:10,11). Jesus came to live with us and to save us. **Jesus** is the reason for our joy at Christmastime and all through the year.

Stretching Further:

With the children, select the Christmas cards that show scenes, people and messages about the birth of Jesus. Cut or tear off the front of each card. Arrange and paste them onto a poster board, about 22 by 28 inches. Attach a loop of yarn or ribbon for hanging the poster in the children's instructional area.

I'm going to give each of you a postcard. This is the size of the first Christmas cards that were printed. Take the card home and think about a drawing that you could make on one side of the card. Make the drawing to send to a friend or a cousin or a grandparent who lives far away. Think about some words to write on the card, too. Maybe you could say, "Good news! Jesus is born," or "Jesus is the reason for Christmas," or "Joy to the world!" Ask a grownup to help you. I'm sure that your card will bring a smile to the person who gets it in the mail.

But first, let's pray: (*Ask children to bow their heads and repeat after you. Say short, meaningful phrases.*)

Dear God, we are happy because you sent Jesus to be a baby, to grow, just like we do. Help us to remember the reason for Christmas. Help us, also, to tell the good news about Jesus to everyone who hasn't heard it. Amen.

(*As children place the extra Christmas cards, handed out earlier, in the basket or box, give each one a postcard.*)

∽

The Greatest Story

Theme: The story of Jesus is the greatest story ever told.

Scripture: . . . go and make followers of all the people in the world. — Matthew 28:19a (NCV)

Preparation: Read Matthew 1:18–2:15, Matthew 28:19–20. Obtain a Nativity Set or artist's rendition to display.

Who likes to hear stories? Do you know what the people in a story are called? They are called characters. Sometimes animals are characters in stories, too. Are the characters in your favorite stories real or make-believe?

I know a story that is the most important story that was ever told or written. Do you know what it is? It's the story of a person named Jesus.

In a story, each happening is called a scene. Here is a scene from Jesus' life story. (*Refer to Nativity scene*). Can you name the characters? What is happening in this scene? Where is it happening?

The story of Jesus says that God is his father. He was born to Mary and Joseph and laid in a manger in the little town of Bethlehem. Angels came to shepherds in the fields who then went to see the baby. Wise men followed a star to find him and bring him gifts.

Then Mary and Joseph took Jesus to Egypt to escape the ruler who wanted to kill him.

That's the story we hear at Christmastime. But it's not the end of the story. What else do you know about Jesus? Did he remain a baby? . . . The baby Jesus grew to be a man. He taught people to love God and to love one another. He made sick people well. He did many miracles so that people would believe he is the Son of God.

Do you think everyone believed him? . . . No, they didn't. Because he claimed that God is his father, Jesus was put to death on a cross.

But Jesus' dying is still not the end of the story. What story about Jesus do we hear at Eastertime? . . . On Easter we celebrate Jesus' leaving his grave! He lives and, even today, he sits beside God the Father in heaven. He gave his life so that, if we believe in him, we can live forever with him in heaven. That's why the story of Jesus is the greatest, most important story ever told. And Jesus is real. He's not a make-believe character in a made-up story.

But he hasn't left us alone. He sends the Holy Spirit to live inside us. Jesus said, (*Matthew 20:b*) "You can be sure I will be with you always. I will continue with you until the end of the world." He will be with us until the end of time! What a wonderful promise!

And Jesus gave us a job to do. Do you know what that job is? It is to obey his teachings and to tell his story to those who haven't heard it. Jesus said, (*Read from Bible Matthew 28:19–20a*) "So go and make followers of all people in the world. . . . Teach them to obey everything I have told you."

How can you help others to learn about Jesus? (*Invite playmates or classmates to participate in Sunday School, Summer Bible School, Christmas programs, children's choir, etc.*)

Let's pray.

Dear God, thank you for Jesus. Let us never get tired of hearing his story. Help us to tell it over and over again. Amen.

Stretching Further:

Jesus also told his disciples to "baptize (the followers) in the name of the Father and the Son and the Holy Spirit." (Matthew 28:19b). Do you know if you have been baptized? You can talk about it with your parents.

~

More About Jesus

Theme: God's word continues to teach us.

Scripture: She (*Mary*) will give birth to a son. You (*Joseph*) will name the son Jesus. . . . All this happened to make clear the full meaning of what the Lord had said through the prophet. —Matthew 1:20b,22

Preparation: Read the prophecies of Jesus' birth in Isaiah 7:14; Isaiah 9:6; Isaiah 61:1–2; Micah 5:2; and the wise men's visit in Matthew 2:1–12.

I already know that you like to hear stories. Does anyone like to read stories? Do you have a favorite story that you never get tired of?

There are stories in the Bible that you will hear many times. Can you think of a Bible story that you have heard more than once?

How do you feel when you hear a Bible story for the second or third time? Are you excited to say, "Oh, I know that story. I know what happened. I know how that story ends!" Or do you think *Oh, no. Not that story again*?

I discovered something about hearing and reading Bible stories. I found that I can learn something new and surprising about a story I thought I already knew.

You know the Bible story we always hear when we are getting ready for Christmas. What is the Christmas story about?

We find the story about Jesus being born in the part of the Bible we call the Gospel of Matthew. The very first page of this book is where the Christmas story begins. This story is one of the Bible stories that people know best.

Here are some things I didn't know about the Christmas story when I was your age.

About 700 years before Jesus was born there lived a man named Isaiah. Isaiah was a prophet. Do you know what a prophet is? A prophet is someone God gives messages to share. God gave Isaiah some very special news that he told all the people. He said that God's Son would be born on earth.

Another prophet lived at about the same time as Isaiah, long, long before Jesus was born. His name was Micah. Micah's message told where the one who would become the King of the Jews would be born. Do you know the name of the person we call the King of the Jews? (*Jesus*) Where was Jesus born? (*in Bethlehem*)

It was because teachers had read Micah's message from God that the wise men knew exactly where to find the baby Jesus. The wise men had also discovered a new star in the sky. They believed that a new star was a sign that a great leader was going to be born. So they followed the star to find him and to give him gifts.

The story about Jesus being born is a story we need to hear over and over again. It is the beginning of the greatest story ever told. It should be at the center of our Christmas celebration. We can always learn something new from the Bible about it. I have learned that, long before Jesus was born, God had told certain messengers that the Son would be born on earth, where he would be born, and that he would become the King of the Jews. I hope you know more about Jesus now, too.

Let's pray.

Dear God, thank you for Jesus. You sent him as a baby at just the right time. Help us to keep on learning new things from the Bible. Especially, help us learn more about Jesus. Amen.

Stretching Further: Read aloud Luke 4:14–21: Jesus reads the words of Isaiah in the synagogue. Talk about Isaiah's words coming true.

∼

A Mighty Fortress

Theme: God can keep us safe.

Scripture: God alone is the mighty rock that keeps me safe, and he is the fortress where I feel secure.—Psalm 62:2 (CEV)

Preparation: 1. Make two cards, large enough for the group to see. With a dark marker, on one card print **fort**, on the second card print **fortress**. 2. Obtain and print online photos of various sizes of snow forts.

We've had lots of snow this winter, haven't we? Do you like to play in the snow? What do you like to do in the snow? (Go sled-riding, tubing, build a snowman, make snowballs . . .) Do you know what a snow fort is? Have you ever helped to make a snow fort? How do you make/build a snow fort? (Can use a big pile of snow and dig into it to make a room like a cave, or pile big snowballs or blocks of snow on top of one another to make a wall.) (*Show photos.*) What do you do with a snow fort after it's finished? (Hide behind it if someone throws a snowball at you in a snowball battle . . .) It can keep you from getting hit, keep you safe. It can be your own special place to go to.

Do you think we can find anything about a fort in the Bible? (*Show first word card.*) This is what the word "fort" looks like. It's a short word. "Fort" means "strong." (*Show second card.*) If we add four more letters, it says "fortress." A fortress is a strong place.

Listen to what David wrote in Psalm 62: *God alone is the mighty rock that keeps me safe, and he is the fortress where I feel secure. God saves me and honors me. He is the mighty rock where I find safety. Trust God, my friends, and always tell him each of your concerns. God is our place of safety.*

Who do you go to when you skin your knee or get a splinter or you have a problem? You go to someone who's bigger and stronger, don't you? So we can go to our Father in heaven. He is the strong fort, the fortress that protects us. We sometimes sing a song that says "A mighty fortress is our God."

David tells us that God is like a mighty rock that keeps us safe. God is our fortress, our place of safety. God is our shelter, our protection, our defense against our enemies. Our God is much, much stronger than a snow fort. God is stronger than anyone or or anything.

So we don't need to be angry or worried or afraid. We can be happy because God, our fortress, is in control. God will take care of us and keep us safe.

Stretching Further: There are several places in the Bible that tell us that God is our defense. Here's another one: (*Read Psalm 46:1*) "God is our mighty fortress, always ready to help us in times of trouble." Did you notice that both verses from the Psalms used the word *always*?

Let's think about Psalms 46:1. (*Read it again*) What does the Psalmist say God is? What does God always do? Let's say the verse together. . . I hope you will *always* remember it.

Let's go to God now. Please bow your heads.

Dear God, thank you for being our fort, our safe place. Help us to trust in you all the time. We know that you love us. We love you, too. We pray in Jesus' name. Amen.

~

Running Out

Theme: God never runs out of love.

Scripture: O give thanks to the Lord, for he is good, for his steadfast love endures forever. —Psalm 136:1

Preparation: Bookmark Psalm 136:1 in your Bible. *Add or substitute your own appropriate experience or anecdote.

---

*Something funny happened at my house. My husband was on the floor playing with our four-year-old grandson. Steven looked at the top of Grandpa's head and said, "Grandpa, are you running out of hair?"

We laughed. Now, we know it isn't kind to make fun of someone. In the Bible there is a story about Elisha, a man who spoke God's word to the people. Some young people laughed at Elisha and called him a baldhead. Do you know what happened to those young people? Two bears came out of the woods and attacked them (2 Kings 2:23,24).

When my family laughed, my husband knew we weren't making fun of him. We laughed at the words that Steven used. We had never thought about hair as something that runs out.

I began thinking about other things that we can run out of. Did you ever run so hard or so long that you had to stop because

17

you were running out of breath? What other things can we run out of? (*time, gasoline, patience, energy, paper, ink for a printer, water, ideas, money, etc.*)

In the gospel of John we read about Jesus being at a wedding party. The people who gave the party ran out of wine for their guests to drink. Jesus' mother told him about the problem. Do you know what Jesus did? He helped by turning water into wine.

That story shows us what God is like. God wants to help. God loves us. We will never have to worry that God will run out of love. That's because God's love comes from a place that will never run dry.

The story of God's love never ends. Another part of the Bible, Psalm 136, tells about God's endless love. The first verse says, (*Read from Bible*) "O give thanks to the Lord, for he is good, for his steadfast love endures forever."

I'm going to say some words that I wrote after I read all twenty-six verses of that psalm. After each time I speak, I want you to say, "Your love is forever." We'll take turns talking to God. This will be our prayer, so please bow your heads.

First I'm going to say, "Thank you, God." You say, "Your love is forever." (*Continue as follows*)

Leader: You alone do great miracles.

Children: Your love is forever.

Leader: You made the heavens and the earth.

Children: Your love is forever.

Leader: You made the sun and moon and stars.

Children: Your love is forever.

Leader: You give food to every living creature.

Children: Your love is forever.

Leader: Thank you, God.

Children: Your love is forever.

Leader: Amen.

Remember that God never runs out of love.

Stretching Further: Do you know people who need help because they have run out of something they need? Perhaps someone at school lost a pencil. If you have two pencils, what could you do? Maybe someone needs a friend. Could you be that friend? Does your family know another family who needs food or money to pay for medicine or rent or heat for their house in winter? How can you and your family show God's love to them?

~

Jesus Reads The Scroll

Theme: Jesus brings good news.

Scripture: "The Spirit of the Lord is upon me, because he has anointed me to bring good news to the poor. He has sent me to proclaim release to the captives and recovery of sight to the blind, to let the oppressed go free, to proclaim the year of the Lord's favor." —Luke 4:18, 19

"The Spirit of the Lord God is upon me; he has sent me to bring good news to the oppressed, to bind up the brokenhearted, to proclaim liberty to the captives, and release to the prisoners; to proclaim the year of the Lord's favor." —Isaiah 61:1–2a

Preparation: To a piece of paper (such as freezer paper) 10 inches by 36 inches, tape an eleven-inch empty paper towel tube to each end to make a scroll. With a broad, dark marker, copy the words of Isaiah 61:1–2a in the middle of the scroll. Roll each end toward the middle. Tie together with a 24-inch cord or shoelace.

Bring several Bibles in various sizes.

Let's look at some Bibles today. (*If a Bible is displayed nearby, call attention to it.*) I brought a smaller Bible that uses words that make it easier for boys and girls to understand. Here's an even smaller Bible. Bibles come in many different sizes.

Has the Bible always been a book like the ones we have today? No. Long ago, in the time of Moses, a part of our Bible was written on tablets of stone. We call those words the "Ten Commandments."

In the time when Jesus lived as a man on earth, the words of God were written on scrolls. Do you know what a scroll is? Scrolls were usually made of sheets of paper or leather fastened together to make a long strip. Wooden rollers were attached to each end. To read what was written on the scroll, the reader had to unroll it. I made a simple scroll to show you. (*Show scroll.*)

In our Bible reading for today, in the Gospel According to Luke, Jesus had come back to Nazareth, the town where he grew up. He went to the synagogue, the place where people met to study the word of God. It was his habit to go to the synagogue every Sabbath Day, just as we go to church every Sunday.

Jesus had been gone from Nazareth for a long time, so asking him to read was like saying to him, "Welcome home." The man in charge handed him the scroll of the prophet Isaiah. Jesus unrolled it and read *(Read from homemade scroll)* "The Spirit of the Lord is upon me, because he has anointed me to bring good news to the poor. He has sent me to proclaim release to the captives and recovery of sight to the blind, to let the oppressed go free, to proclaim the year of the Lord's favor" (Isaiah 61:1,2a).

Jesus knew that these words that Isaiah had written more than 700 years earlier were about him. So he sat down and said, "What you have just heard me read has come true today." He was saying, "I am the one who will help set people free. I bring good news. I will make this good news happen. I *am* the good news."

God sent Jesus as a gift to everyone, and especially to those who are poor, hurting, and sad. Jesus sent his disciples to tell the good news, too. And he wants each one of us to share the good news that we read in the Bible. How can you do that? Do you have a neighbor, a friend, or a classmate who doesn't know about Jesus? Maybe, if you talk with your parents about it, you could invite that person to come to Sunday School and church with you to learn the good news.

Stretching Further: Arrange beforehand for a specific project that will involve the children in providing Bibles or helping others near or far.

Let's pray:

> Dear God, thank you for loving us so much that you gave us your son, Jesus. Help us to be brave to tell the good news to those who don't know it. We pray in Jesus' name. Amen.

～

Follow The Leader

Theme: All who follow Jesus are winners.

Scripture: Jesus said . . . "Follow me."—Luke 9:59a

Preparation: Bookmark Luke 9:59. On 3 x 5-inch index cards (one per child), use a dark marker to print Join **God's winning team. Follow Jesus.** Add "happy face" stickers.

Have you ever played a game called Follow the Leader? How do you play that game? Let's have some fun. I'm going to be your leader. Follow me and do what I do. (*Walk around the congregation, clapping your hands or saying, "Jesus loves me," "Jesus loves you, too," [point to congregation] or other appropriate words. Then be seated.*)

Were you a leader or a follower? Is it easier to lead or to follow? In the Bible (*Open to Luke 9:59*) we read that Jesus said, "Follow me." When we played Follow the Leader, you saw me, so you knew what to do. But how can we follow Jesus if we can't see him? The Bible tells us how Jesus lived and how much he loves us. Jesus told us to be kind, to love one another, and to obey God's commandments. When we do that and trust him, we are following Jesus.

In most games there are winners. If it's a game with teams, would you rather be on the winning team or the other team? In the

Bible, Jesus invites all of us to be part of God's winning team. We can learn to do winning things like telling the truth and helping one another, and then we will be following Jesus.

Another way to be sure we are following Jesus is to talk with him. How can we do that? Do you know that Jesus is the only person in the Bible who invites us to pray in his name? He is always ready to help us to follow him whenever, wherever, and however we pray.

Let's pray now. Please bow your heads and repeat after me.

Dear Jesus, we want you to be our leader. Help us to follow you every day. Help us to be kind and to love one another. We pray in your name. Amen.

Stretching Further:

How can **you** be a good **leader**? If you act the way Jesus showed us, you are showing others how he lived, too. How does Jesus want us to act? (*Review: being kind and good, helping one another, sharing, telling the truth, trying to get along well with others, obeying your parents and teachers, etc.*) When another person copies what you do, you are not only a follower of Jesus, you have become a leader, too. You are leading others to Jesus.

Before you leave, I have a reminder to give you. (*Give out index cards with message.*) It says, "Join God's winning team. Follow Jesus." Remember: You are a winner if you follow Jesus.

∽

Jesus Tells A Story

Theme: Love God and your neighbor.

Scripture: . . . Love the Lord your God with all your heart, and with all your soul, and with all your strength, and with all your mind; and your neighbor as yourself.—Luke 10:27

Preparation: 1. Read Luke 10:25–37.* 2. Practice saying Luke 10:27 with motions.** 3. Print the passage from Luke 10:27 on individual index cards to give to the children. 4. For "STRETCHING FURTHER," find online the song *Won't You Be My Neighbor?* as sung by "Mr. Rogers" on TV. If you plan to use it, give the music to the pianist or song leader beforehand.

Who likes to hear stories? What kind of stories do you like? (*true stories or "made-up" stories; stories about animals; mysteries; scary stories; tall tales; stories with happy endings?*)

Where might you hear a story being told? (*at home, in your bedroom, by a campfire, in school or church, on television or radio*) Who might tell a story? (*teacher, parent or grandparent, babysitter, scout leader, preacher*)

Do you know that Jesus was a storyteller, too? He knew that people like to hear stories. Lots of people came to hear his stories.

When Jesus talked outside, people sat with their families on a grassy hillside or on a beach to listen to him.

One story* that Jesus told is about a man who was going down a road when some robbers jumped out and beat him. They took his money and his clothes and left him lying there alone beside the road. He was badly hurt and bleeding.

Another man came along. This man was a priest. His work was to teach people abbout God's love and God's ways. Yet, when the priest saw the man who was hurt, he didn't stop to help him.

A second man came down the road. He was a helper to the priests who worked in the temple. He stopped and looked at the man who had been beaten. Then he, too, walked away without doing anything to help him.

A third man was traveling down that road. He lived in a faraway place called Samaria, so he was called a Samaritan. The Samaritan saw the man lying there and went over to him. He stopped his bleeding, cleaned his cuts and put bandages on them. Then he lifted the man onto his own donkey's back and took him to an inn. There he paid for a bed and food and drink for him. The Samaritan gave the innkeeper more money to take care of the injured man. He told the innkeeper, "If you spend more than I've given you, I'll pay you on my way back."

After Jesus finished telling this story, he asked, "Which of these three men do you think was a neighbor to the man who was attacked by robbers?" How would you answer Jesus' question? Which man do you think acted like a good neighbor?. . . It was not the man who lived next door.

Jesus said, "Go and do the same." (Luke 10:37a CEV) When he told the story of the good Samaritan, Jesus meant that our neighbors are not just the people who live near us or who look like us and talk like us. Everyone is our neighbor.

The Bible verse that begins the story that Jesus told goes like this: (*Quote Luke 10:27, using motions and encouraging the children to do the same.*)**

Love the Lord your God (*point upward*) **with all your heart** (*place right hand over heart*), **and with all your soul** (*keep right* *hand over heart and place left hand over right side of chest*), **and with all your strength** (*flex arm muscles*), **and with all your mind** (*place both hands on forehead*); **and your neighbor** (*outstretch both arms*) **as yourself** (*bring both hands to chest, one hand over the other*).

I think Luke 10:27 is a good verse to remember. Let's try it again. (*Repeat*)

And we can use that verse as a prayer, too. Let's bow our heads and pray:

Dear God, help me to love you with all my heart, and with all my soul, and with all my strength, and with all my mind. Help me to love my neighbor as I love myself. In Jesus' name. Amen.

Here's a card to help you remember what Jesus commanded us to do. I hope you'll practice saying the verse and doing what it says during the week ahead. (*Hand out cards.*)

Stretching Further: Tell about "Mr. Rogers" who always began his TV show for children by singing "Won't You Be My Neighbor?" Say the words; then sing the song.

∽

Magic Or Miracles?

Theme: Jesus does miracles, not magic.

Scripture: Jesus did this, the first of his signs . . . and revealed his glory; and his disciples believed in him.—John 2:11

Preparation: Read John 2:1–11: The Wedding at Cana.

Our story from the Bible today is about a wedding. Have you ever been to a wedding? After the couple is married, how do people usually celebrate? (*by having a party, eating and drinking together, dancing, giving gifts*)

Jesus had been invited to this wedding. Everyone was having a happy time. They ate good food, and they drank wine. Wine is a drink made from grapes. But Jesus' mother noticed a problem: the family had run out of wine. The party was about to be ruined. The bridegroom was going to be embarrassed.

She told Jesus about the problem, and Jesus turned jars of water into wine.

When I was getting ready for this lesson, I thought about putting some powdered drink mix into the bottom of a pitcher that you couldn't see through. Then, when I poured water into the pitcher it would be a grape drink.

But that would be a trick, and I didn't want to trick you.

Jesus didn't perform tricks. He was not a magician.

When Jesus turned water into wine, he worked a miracle. Only God can make miracles happen. Jesus and God are one.

What Jesus did at the wedding was the first of many miracles that he performed. He healed sick people, he brought dead people back to life, he walked on water, he fed more than 5,000 people with five loaves of bread and two fish.

He did all these miracles to help people. And he did them so that people would believe he is God's Son who had come to save them. In the Book of John we read "Jesus did this, the first of his signs . . . and revealed his glory; and his disciples believed in him." (John 2:11)

Jesus still works miracles in the hearts and lives of people who believe in him.

I believe. Do you?

Let's pray:

Dear God, thank you for sending your Son Jesus to love us and to save us. Amen.

Stretching Further:

Read and talk about another miracle that Jesus performed, such as Luke 5:4–11. What did Simon Peter, James and John do after they caught so many fish? (*They left everything and followed Jesus.*) How can you follow Jesus? (*by being loving and kind and helping one another; by telling others about Jesus*)

∼

He Is Risen!

Theme: Jesus is alive.

Scripture: This is the day the Lord has made. Let us rejoice and be glad today. —Psalm 118:24 (NCV)

Preparation: Obtain pom-poms or streamers for each child to wave.

Good morning! (*Read from Bible.*) Verse 24 of Psalm 118 says, "This is the day the Lord has made. Let us rejoice and be glad today!"

Is anyone glad today? Why are you happy today?

At the bookstore I saw lots of books with Easter in their titles. There were books about the Easter bunny, egg hunts, the Easter parade, Easter baskets, Easter surprises. I even saw a book about an Easter beagle!

Do you know which story is the best Easter story of all? The most important Easter story is about Jesus. Jesus had died and his body had been put into a cave, called a tomb. Do you know what happened to Jesus on the day we call Easter? When Mary Magdalene went to take care of his dead body, he wasn't there. She saw him alive, standing outside the cave! He talked to her.

Mary was so happy that she ran to tell his friends that Jesus was alive! He had risen from the dead. What wonderful good news!

Even today on Easter morning we celebrate Jesus' being alive. Since that first Easter morning, people who believe in Jesus Christ have greeted one another, not by saying "Good morning," or "Hello," but by saying, "Christ is risen!" And the people being greeted have answered, "He is risen indeed!"

Let's greet the rest of the people here this morning. Let's stand up and shout, "Christ is risen!" (*If children don't shout enthusiastically, encourage them to repeat the message.*)

Congregation, let's hear you shout, "He is risen indeed!" (*Repeat several times. If pom-poms or streamers are available, hand them to the children. Lead them around the sanctuary, waving and shouting.*)

Let's pray.

Dear God, thank you that Jesus is not dead. No! He is alive. He lives with you in heaven. And, if we believe in him, and invite him in, he lives in our hearts today. Alleluia! Amen.

Stretching Further:

Teach the song, "God's Not Dead" (*Sing-a-long Songbook 3*. PO Box 851622, Mobile, AL 36685–1622: Integrity Music, Inc., 1993. See online: amazon music Just for Kids Sing-a-long Songbook 3). If the music is not available, use the words as a chant with suitable motions (clapping hands, stomping feet, etc.).

Alternate Stretching Further:

Read John 14:19b: Because I live, you will live too. (NCV)

This is a promise that Jesus made to everyone who believes in him. That means that you, too, can live forever with him in heaven.

∼

The Lord Is My Banner

Theme: Let us be a nation under God.

Scripture: And Moses built an altar and called it, The Lord is my banner. —Exodus 17:15

Preparation: If the national flag is not available in the room, bring a small one. Be sure to treat it respectfully. If the Christian flag is not on display, bring a photograph of it, which can be found by searching Christian flag online.

I've seen a lot of flags in the last week. Have you noticed them, too?

Why have people hung out their flags? . . . Because the flag reminds us that we are a free people, and many men and women have fought in wars for our freedom. On the fourth day of July many years ago some brave men in this country signed a paper saying they would be free from obeying the laws of another country. This new country would make laws fair to everyone. (*Adapt to the country and the day, such as Memorial Day, Flag Day, etc.*)

In some places we see the American flag at all times of the year. I'm thinking of places where sports are played, sports like baseball, basketball and football,. Before the games begin, our national anthem— our song— the "Star-Spangled Banner," is sung. Banner is another word for flag.

Do you think the Bible says anything about flags or banners? In the book of Exodus, Chapter 17, verse 15, we read that God's people, the Israelites, had been fighting their enemies. The Israelites won the battle. Then Moses built an altar to God. He named that place where they worshiped God "The Lord is my Banner."

Have you noticed the American flag here in our church? Point to it.

Have you learned to say the Pledge of Allegiance to the American flag? A pledge of allegiance is a promise to be true to what the country and its flag stand for. If you know it, say it with me now. "**I pledge Allegiance to the flag of the United States of America and to the Republic for which it stands, one Nation under God, indivisible, with liberty and justice for all.**"

Did you notice the words "one Nation under God"? Our faith in God is our greatest strength.

Have you noticed another flag also? It's called the Christian flag. What do you see on this flag? The red cross helps us to remember how Jesus died; he gave his blood for us on the cross so we are free from being punished for the wrongs we've done. Most of the flag is white. Because of what Jesus did for us, we are washed clean, as white as snow. The blue color means that we are true to what Jesus taught.

The Christian flag is not the flag of any country or nation. It belongs to all people everywhere who follow Jesus Christ.

Long ago Moses named the altar "The Lord is my Banner" because he knew that it is God who gives us power and strength. Depending on God is like following the banner of God. That means obeying God's rules and going where God leads us.

Did you know there is also a pledge to the Christian flag? It goes like this: **I pledge allegiance to the Christian flag and to the Savior for whose kingdom it stands; One brotherhood, uniting all true Christians in service and love.** (*Then have children stand straight and tall, face the flag, place right hand over heart, and repeat after you. The congregation may also want to join in.*)

Stretching Further:

If the flag (or a photograph) of your church's denomination is available, show it and talk about the meaning of its symbols.

Now whenever you see an American flag, I hope you will think of the Christian flag, too. And remember Moses saying, "The **Lord** is my Banner."

Let's pray:

Dear God, thank you that we can live in this free country. Let it truly be a "nation under God." Help us to follow your banner of love, and go where you want us to go, and do what you want us to do, in the name of Jesus. Amen.

∼

Our Father's Day

Theme: We are a part of God's family.

Scripture: But to all who received him, who believed in his name, he gave power to become children of God.—John 1:12

Preparation: Bring enough 5" x 8" index cards so that each child may receive two; a broad-tipped marker; and several examples of Father's Day cards: serious, humorous, and a home-made one without words.

Today is Father's Day, a day when we give special attention to our fathers. Maybe you don't have a father here. Maybe your father doesn't live with you. Perhaps you have an uncle, a grandfather, or a special friend who spends time with you. What will you do that will make your father, grandfather, or good friend happy?

Will you give him a special card today? I brought some cards to show you. (*Show and read cards' messages.*) Here's one that I made, but I didn't write any words on it. If you made a card for your dad, what words would you like to write on it?

(*Use the marker to write "Love" in large letters inside the card.*) Who can read this word? When we look at the letters l-o-v-e, we say "love." But do you know that l-o-v-e isn't really love? We call those letters symbols. When we see them together, they make us think of love. We can write and say the word "love," but what we *do* is even more important than what we *write* or what we *say*. Real love is listening, doing what you're told to do, helping, sharing and giving. Love is making your bed, putting away your toys, helping to set the table, or taking out the garbage. These are some things we can do to show that we love our fathers and our mothers.

Who was Jesus' father? His father on earth was Joseph. Joseph took care of Jesus. He showed Jesus how to work with wood, to be a carpenter like himself.

Jesus called someone else besides Joseph his Father. Do you know who? It was God. When Jesus' disciples asked him to teach them to pray, he said (*Read from Matthew 6:9*), "This . . . is how you should pray: 'Our Father in heaven, hallowed be your name . . . '" Notice that Jesus didn't say they should pray to "my Father" in heaven. He said, "Our Father." And the word of God also says (*Read John 1:12*), " . . . to all who received him, who believed in his name, he gave power to become children of God." So if we believe in Jesus, we are a part of God's family. God is our Father in heaven, too.

So, what can we do to make our Father God happy? To show that we love our Father in heaven, we thank God for all the good things he gives us. We sing songs of praise. We hear or read God's word and we listen and obey. We show how much we love God by the way we treat other people, with kindness—the way we want to be treated.

Should you give special attention to your father only one day in a year? No. You should show that you love your father every day and, not only your father here, but, especially God, your Father in heaven.

Stretching Further: Tell the story that Jesus told about a son who asked his father for his share of the father's money, left home and spent the money foolishly, and finally had to go back to his father. (Luke 15:11–24) How is the father in the story like our Father God? (*God loves his children, waits patiently for them to come back after doing wrong, forgives, and celebrates their return.*)

After we pray, I'm going to give each of you two cards. Maybe you've already given your dad a Father's Day card, but that's all right. I'm sure he will like another one, especially if you make it. At home you can draw a picture on one side of it. It could be a picture of your family. It might show things that your dad or your special friend enjoys: a fishing rod, a golf club, a basketball hoop and a ball, a boat, a camera, a musical instrument, or a tent. On the other side you could write, or ask someone to help you write "Love" or "I love you" or "Thank you" and sign your name.

Guess what I'm going to ask you to do with the other card. Do you think your Father in heaven likes to see your drawings? Does God like you to say "I love you" and "Thank you"? Yes. You can make a drawing of what God has made, like a rainbow, flowers, birds, trees, mountains, waterfalls, the ocean, and your family. God will see it and your card will make God happy.

It also makes your Father in heaven happy when we pray. We can pray at any time of day or night because God is always listening. Let's talk to God now. Please bow your heads and repeat after me.

Our Father God, we thank you for caring for us and loving us. Thank you for the fathers and grandfathers you gave us. Thank you for sending us your son, Jesus. We know that we are your children, too. We love you. We pray in Jesus' name. Amen.

(*Give two index cards to each child.*)

∽

Keeping Cool

Theme: We need spiritual food every day.

Scripture: I am the bread of life.—John 6:48

Preparation: Gather several large color photographs of polar bears and seals. They can be found online by searching polar bear photos and ringed seal photos.

It's been very hot, hasn't it? Do you like being outside when it's hot?

Sometimes I think it's too hot, and I want to be somewhere where it's cool, and have a drink of cold water.

I brought some pictures to help us to think about cooler weather. (*Show a picture of polar bears in snow.*) Do you know what kind of animals these are? Do they look cool?

*Last fall I went on a long trip to the Hudson Bay in Canada where polar bears live. I learned a lot about polar bears on my visit. One thing that bears do is called hibernating. Do you know what a bear does when it hibernates? A bear rests or sleeps when it hibernates. What time of year do animals usually hibernate?

I learned that polar bears hibernate during the summer. Why do you think they do that? Do you know what polar bears eat? (*Show photograph of a seal.*) They eat seals. These seals look small on the picture, but they can grow to be six feet long—longer than

I am tall. The seals live on or under the ice. (*Show polar bear lying down on the ice, waiting for a seal to come up for air.*)

Guess what happens to the ice in the bay in July when it's hot. When the ice melts, the bears have to come onto the land, where there are no seals for them to eat. So the bears dig dens in the ground and hibernate in summer. Right now they are in their dens, resting and keeping cool until the weather turns very cold, and the water freezes, and they can go out on the ice again to hunt seals.

The polar bears actually have a "walking hibernation." They come out of their dens sometimes and look for berries or seaweed or mussels to eat. But most of the time from July to October or November, for about three months, they don't eat. Do you think you could live from, say, the Fourth of July when we have fireworks, until the leaves change colors in the fall, without eating?

Who made the first polar bears? (*Show the Bible and open it to Genesis 1.*) The Bible tells us, on the first page of the first book, "God made the wild animals of the earth of every kind" (Genesis 1:25a). Who made the first people? The Bible tells us that God created humankind, or human beings—that means people (Genesis 1:27a). And God saw, or looked at everything that God had made, and it was very good (Genesis 1:31a).

So God made the polar bears so that they can live for a very long time without eating. But God didn't make us that way. We should eat every day. What are your favorite things to eat? Does anyone like to eat bread? A peanut butter and jelly sandwich?

There's another kind of food that we need. I call it spiritual food—food for the spirit, food for that part of ourselves we sometimes call our heart or soul. We need this kind of food every day, too. Jesus called himself "the bread of life" (John 6:48–51). And Jesus said that anyone who eats this bread will live forever.

How can we get this bread that Jesus gives? We get it when we believe in Jesus; when we pray—talking to God and listening; when we read the Bible or listen to Bible stories; when we learn about God in church and Sunday School; when we sing about

Jesus; and when we talk with our parents and teachers and friends about him.

Let's have some food for our spirit right now. (*Ask children to bow their heads and repeat after you. Say short, meaningful phrases.*)

Dear God, we thank you for making polar bears and seals and us. Thank you for good food to eat. Thank you for the Bible and for Jesus, the bread of life. Help us to find food for our spirit every day. We pray in Jesus' name. Amen.

Stretching Further:

Read John 4:31–34 to see what Jesus said about his spiritual food (*doing the will and work of his Father, bringing people to God*). Note that we are fed and we grow, not only by what we take in, but also by what we give out for God. Ask "What can you do for God?"

~

A Leg To Stand On

Theme: God's good creation teaches about God.

Scripture: How many are your works, O Lord! In wisdom you made them all; the earth is full of your creatures.—Psalm 104:24 (NIV)

Preparation: Bring a pink plastic flamingo or a large photo of one. Photos can be found online by searching flamingo photos. Obtain the words and music for "All Things Bright and Beautiful." Words: Cecil Francis Alexander, 1848 (Gen. 1:31); Music: 17th cent. English melody, arr. by Martin Shaw, 1915.

See what I brought to show you today. (*Show flamingo or photo.*) Do you know what this is? * In the room where I study the Bible with other grown-ups I found twenty-five of these birds leaning against the wall. I learned that a few years ago the youth of the church had used these flamingos to make money for a mission trip. People could pay the youth to put a flamingo in a family's yard during the night so they would be surprised to see it when they woke up. Or, if someone didn't want to have a flamingo put in his yard, he could give money so it would not appear there. It was a fun way to raise money for a good cause.

Actually, a pink plastic flamingo is one of the most famous lawn ornaments in the United States. It was first made more than sixty years ago. In a prank at the University of Wisconsin, a hill covered with more than 1,000 flamingos greeted the college students on the first day of classes in 1979.

I wanted to know more about real flamingos. What do you know about this bird? (*Allow time for responses.*)

Who created the first flamingo to live on earth? In the book of Genesis we read that God created "every living thing" and "every winged bird according to its kind"—Genesis 1:21.

God made every kind of creature special. Here are some ways that God made the flamingo special. One way is how this bird rests. When you get tired and need to rest, how do you like to rest? Do you sit? Do you lie down? On your back? On your side? Or on your stomach? Maybe you like to curl up with a stuffed animal.

Do you think you could sleep standing up? Standing on one leg? That's what the flamingo does. Curling one leg under its body keeps its foot and body warm in cold water.

Can you eat while you're standing? Sitting? While you're upside down? The Caribbean flamingo eats with its head upside down. In this position it sucks water and mud through special filters in its bill. Then it swallows shrimp and other small water creatures that are left.

Did you notice that a flamingo's legs are longer than its body? (*Say, "Touch your ankle."*) The flamingo's ankle is halfway up its legs. (*Say, "Touch your knee."*) The flamingo's knee is close to its body. There are many more, interesting things to learn about this beautiful, colorful bird. The flamingo is unique—very unusual.

I think that God must have had lots of fun making this wonderful bird and all the other living things. In Psalm 104:24 we read "How many are your works, O Lord! In wisdom you made them all; the earth is full of your creatures." And in Genesis 1:21 we read "And God saw that it (God's creation) was good." God's creatures help us to see how good and wise and powerful God is. Each creature is special (unique), and each of you is special.

There is no one else just like you. And God loves you.

Stretching Further:

Sing "All Things Bright and Beautiful."

Let us thank God the Creator.

How wise you are, O God. Thank you for beautiful birds and for all the living things that you have made. Thank you for making each of your creatures unique and good, even me. Amen.

As you leave this place of worship today, be sure to look around you at all of the wonderful things that God has made. You might want to say thank you again.

~

Jesus Says

Theme: Jesus teaches us how to live.

Scripture: I am the way, and the truth, and the life.—John 14:6a

Preparation: Use a Bible with Jesus' words printed in red or in a different type of print.

Let's play a game today. You know how to play Simon Says, don't you? I will tell you to do something, but don't do it unless I first say "Simon says" to do it. Let's try it. (*Give directions for simple activities, one at a time, such as* **stand up; clap two times; turn around; touch your nose; sit down,** *etc. Unless you say* **"Simon says stand up,"** *the children should not obey the command.*) It's fun to play Simon Says. Simon can tell us to do almost anything, can't he?

But what Simon says is not nearly as important as what Jesus says to us, is it? Have you ever wondered what Jesus might say? We have a way to learn what Jesus said. How can we do that? The Bible tells us what Jesus said at certain times and places. Many of the people who listened called him "teacher." They wanted to hear what he said and to learn from him.

To make it easier for us to learn what Jesus said, in this Bible (*show open Bible*) his words are printed in red ink instead of black ink. Let's see what you already know about what Jesus said. I'm going to read some sentences. If you think Jesus said it, nod your head up and down and say, "Jesus says." If you think Jesus didn't say it, shake your head from side to side and say, "No-o-o-o" (or "No way").

Let's try a sentence together. "If someone hits you, hit that person back harder." Did Jesus say that? N-o-o-o-o. What Jesus said was the opposite. "If anyone strikes you on the cheek, offer the other also." (Luke 6:29)

Let's try some more sentences. (*Continue with the following statements, as time permits.*)

1. "Go, and I will follow you." —**No-o-o-o.** Jesus said, "Follow me." (Mark 1:17)

2. "Do to other people before they do something to you." —**No-o-o-o.** Jesus said, "Do to others as you would have them do to you." (Luke 6:31)

3. "Love your neighbor as yourself." —**Jesus says.** (Mark 12:31a)

4. "Have faith in being lucky."—**No-o-o-o.** Jesus said, "Have faith in God." (Mark 11:22)

5. "Love your God with all your heart, and with all your soul, and with all your mind, and with all your strength." —**Jesus says.** (Mark 12:30)

6. "I am the way, and the truth, and the life." —**Jesus says.** (John 14:6)

Jesus not only tells us and shows us the way to live, he says that he **is** the way. Jesus is our way, our path, to God the Father. Jesus not only tells the truth, he says he **is** the truth, and he **is** the life. He promises that, if we believe him and believe **in** him, we will live forever with God. What a wonderful promise!

So what should you do when you have a problem and don't know what to do about it? Your parents and Sunday School teachers can help you find in the Bible what Jesus says to do.

And when you are playing Simon Says, remember that it's even more important to pay attention to what *Jesus* says.

Let's pray. Please bow your heads and repeat after me. (*Say short, meaningful phrases.*)**Thank you, God, for sending Jesus to love us and teach us, to tell us and show us the way to live. Help us to do what Jesus says. We pray in his name. Amen.**

Stretching Further: Choose one or more of Jesus' statements to explore, including the context in which Jesus said them.

∾

Spoons

Theme: Love is doing.

Scripture: Dear children, let us not love with words or tongue but with actions and in truth.—I John 3:18 (NIV)

Preparation: Bring two wooden spoons: a new, unused one; a darkened, used spoon. Also bring an assortment of small plastic spoons of various colors, shapes and sizes so that each child may receive one.

All of you look nice this morning. Your clothes are very colorful. Look at the people sitting out there. Don't they look nice, too?

I brought some **things** for you to look at, also. (*Show large wooden spoons.*) Do you know what these are? Take a good look at them. How are these spoons alike? How are they different? Which spoon do you think is older? Why do you think it is darker than the others? It's dark because I've used it many times for mixing good things to eat, like brownies.

Do you think I've used the light-colored spoon for mixing or stirring food? No, this spoon has never been used.

In the Bible, John, a follower of Jesus, wrote about loving one another. Listen: "Dear children, let us not love with words or tongue but with actions and truth." (I John 3:18).

But what do love and spoons have to do with one another? John says we should love, not just with words, but with **action**. Love is **doing**. If I mix and bake some brownies for my family or take them to welcome a new neighbor, I'm doing something kind for someone else. I'm showing love. Jesus told his disciples, "Just as I have loved you, you also should love one another" (John 13:34b).

A new wooden spoon is pretty to look at, but it isn't doing much good if it isn't being used to make something good to eat. So it is with **us**, the people of the church. If we just come in our nice clothes and sit here on Sundays, but don't **do** anything else to help other people, we're like the new spoon that isn't being used. Sometimes we need to get our hands and feet and clothes dirty in doing good work.

God is pleased when we come to worship, to give thanks and sing praises. But I think God is even more pleased when we leave here and **do** the work of the church, to be Jesus' hands, feet, ears, mouth and heart.

But we don't always need a tool like a mixing spoon, a rake, a broom, or a paint brush to do good work. Let's think about some things that **you** can do to show love to someone else. What can you do for your neighbors? (*Help to take care of their pet and plants while they're away.*) For someone who's sick? (*Make a get well card; draw a picture or sing a song to cheer someone up.*) For your play-mates? (*Let someone else go first; share toys; pick up the toys when you're finished playing and put them away.*) What else can you do for others? (*Bring food for the Food Bank; invite someone to come with you to Sunday School or Vacation Bible School, etc.*)

Stretching Further: I brought some small spoons, too. (*Show small plastic spoons.*) What do you notice about these spoons? Are they all the same color? . . . the same size? Are we all alike? Are we different in the kinds of things we're good at doing? . . . in the ways we can show love to other people? After we pray, I'm going to give each of you a spoon to help you to remember to do something loving and unselfish, in your own special way, for someone else today and every day next week.

Praying for God to bless others is something all of us can do, and we don't need any tools to do it. Let's pray now. Please bow your heads and repeat after me.

Dear God, thank you for loving us. We ask your blessing on each person here this morning. Help all of us to be like Jesus. Show us how we can love one another, as he loves us. We pray in his name. Amen.

~

Growing Like Jesus

Theme: God helps me to be more like Jesus.

Scripture: And Jesus increased in wisdom and in years, and in divine and human favor—Luke 2:52.

Preparation: This message is appropriate for use at the beginning of a school year. In a backpack put items that might be used at school, such as crayons, various kinds of lined and unlined paper, markers, a ruler, an eraser, a glue stick, a lunch box or bag. Include enough pencils to give one to each child.

Vacation is over and school will soon begin again. Is anyone going to be starting kindergarten? First grade? Second? Third? Fourth? How about preschool or daycare?

*For most of my life, this time of year for me meant going back to school, too, either as a student or a teacher. I still have some things that I, or someone in my family, used in school. I put them in my backpack to show you. (*Take out lunch box.*) Do you know what this is? Does your lunch bag or box look anything like this? In the stores I saw lunch bags and backpacks made of strong nylon material. They were pink and purple, blue and yellow, orange and black and green. Some had special places to put cold food to keep it cold, or hot food to stay hot. (*Show other items in backpack. Ask children to tell what they are.*)

Going to school is about learning, no matter how old you are. Do you know that teachers are always learning, too? Do you think the Bible tells us anything about learning? One story in the Bible tells about Jesus **teaching** in the temple, instead of being with his parents. Jesus was just twelve years old in that story.

The Bible doesn't tell us any more about him for his next eighteen years except this: (*Read from Bible Luke 2:52*) "Jesus increased in wisdom and in years, and in divine and human favor."

What about that word "increase"? Do you know what happens when something increases? It gets bigger or greater. Jesus increased in wisdom. That means he learned more and he understood what he was learning. He became wiser.

Jesus increased in years. What does that mean? (*He got older, had more birthdays; grew bigger, taller and stronger.*) You may need new clothes now because what you wore last year doesn't fit anymore. Some parents keep a chart that shows how much you weigh and how tall you are on each birthday. Maybe your school nurse will weigh and measure you, too, as you increase in years.

Jesus "increased in divine and human favor." That means that God was pleased with him and so were the people.

It was important that Jesus should grow in wisdom and in years, and that he should please God. So it is important that we should do the same. How can we get wisdom? Learning is just a part of getting wisdom. We can study, ask questions, and learn from books and parents and teachers and the Internet. But wisdom and understanding come from God. Wisdom is a gift from God to us. James, another follower of Jesus, says that if you need wisdom, you should ask God, and God will give it to you. (James 1:5)

(*Note: A later sermon, "BE WISE," expands on the theme of getting wisdom.*)

How do we find favor with God, as Jesus did? How can we please God? If we do good and kind things for other people like Jesus did, that will make God smile and be happy with us. How can we use these things from my backpack to show that we care about someone else? (*lunch box - share food with someone who forgot, or doesn't have a snack or lunch; crayons, markers, pencils, paper - draw a picture, make a card, write a thank you or get well note or an "I love you" to Dad and Mom or "I'm glad you're my teacher to your teacher, write a poem or a story; cut or fold paper to make a figure to give to someone who is sick or who got in trouble*)

What if we used the crayons, markers, or pencils to draw or write on the walls at home or in school or church? Would that please God, your teachers, and your parents? No. What if you wrote something mean or nasty about someone? It's important to learn that some things are **not** good to do because they are unkind and they hurt someone or make them feel bad or sad. Those kinds of things do not please God.

Stretching Further:

Read aloud Luke 2:46,47. What kinds of questions might twelve-year-old Jesus have asked the teachers in the temple? What might the teachers have asked him?

Alternate Stretching Further:

In a following session, have the children do one of the activities suggested above, or an activity suggested by the children to show caring.

I'm going to give each of you a pencil to take with you. I hope this pencil will help you to remember to do something kind and good this week.

But first, let's pray.

Dear God, we want to grow like Jesus. We ask you to fill our minds with wisdom. Let us be ready to do good things every day and in every way. We pray in Jesus' name. Amen.

(*Distribute pencils. Say, "Do something good with your pencil."*)

~

Show and Tell

Theme: Show God's love by loving one another.

Scripture: This . . . is what I command you: love one another.—John 15:17 (TEV)

Preparation: 1. Obtain a cross small enough to handle easily but large enough for all the children to see. 2. Bookmark John 15:17 in your Bible. 3. Optional: Obtain enough small crosses (perhaps made from palm leaves) to give one to each child.

Do you ever do "show and tell" at school or Sunday School? What happens during "show and tell"? Yes, someone brings something to show to everyone, and then she or he tells about it. Have you taken anything to school to show? What did you say about it? Yes, you might tell where the thing came from, what it's made of, how it was made, and why it is special.

Do you know that Jesus liked to show and tell, too? What he brought to show and tell about was God's love. But love isn't something you can put in a box or hold in your hand. So Jesus *showed* us God's love by what he did. He gave to the poor and fed those who were hungry. He blessed children. Jesus healed those who were sick and he made a blind man see. And after his friend Lazarus died, Jesus brought him back to life.

Jesus *told* many stories about how much God loves us. He taught anyone and everyone who would listen. He spoke good, kind words. Jesus taught his disciples how to live and he *told* them to teach people everywhere about God's love for them.

I brought a cross for my "show and tell" today. (*Show cross.*) It's special because Jesus *showed* his love for us by dying on a cross. Why did he do that? He died on the crosss so that we might live forever with him in heaven (I John 4:19). This cross is small and smooth and shiny. The big cross that Jesus carried was not. It was rough and heavy.

Notice that the cross has two parts. This (*vertical*) part points up to God. (*Raise one hand and point upward, asking children to do the same.*) It reminds us that God loves us and we should love God. This (*horizontal*) part of the cross reminds us that God stretches out his arms (*demonstrate and have children stretch out their arms*) and loves everyone in the whole world. And Jesus' arms were stretched out when he hung on the cross. So we should love everyone, too— not just our family and friends and people who look like us and talk like us, but everyone else as well.

In the Bible we read that Jesus commanded (*Read John 15:17*), "Love one another." Do you know what a command is? A command is an order. Jesus didn't say, "Maybe you should try to love one another," or "It might be a good idea to love each other." Jesus commanded us to "Do it," to "Love one another" just as he loves us.

How can you *show* others that you love them? (*Encourage children to respond.*) Some ways that you are already *showing* love are . . . (*Mention Sunday School, Bible School, and church projects in which children participate, such as Food Bank; collecting pennies; donating toys and clothing; making cards for those who are ill; visiting shut-ins; recycling items; etc.*).

I hope you will *show* love however you can and wherever you can and whenever you can. And don't forget to *tell* the stories of Jesus to anyone who might not have heard them. Try starting with a friend.

Stretching Further: Pass the cross to a child while saying, "God loves me and God loves you." The child repeats the words and passes the cross to the next child until everyone has received and given the cross. The last child returns the cross to the teacher.

If available, give each child a small cross to help them to remember that God loves us and we should love God. God loves everyone, and we should love everyone, too.

Let's pray.

Dear God, thank you for sending Jesus to show and tell us about God's love. Help us to do our best to show and tell others about your love, too. May we obey Jesus' command to love one another today and every day. In Jesus' name. Amen.

~

Children As Teachers

Theme: Children can teach about God by their example.

Scripture: (Jesus said) "Let the little children come to me; do not stop them; for it is to such as these that the kingdom of heaven belongs. Truly I tell you, whoever does not receive the kingdom of God as a little child will never enter it" (Mark 10:14.15).

Preparation: 1. On 3" x 5" index cards (one per child) print with dark marker: **My name is _____. I am a teacher.** 2. Bookmark Mark 10:14, 15.

Note: This message is especially appropriate for, or after, a Children's Day program.

I'm wondering today, what do you want to be when you grow up? Does anyone here want to be a bus driver? A cook in a restaurant? A house builder? A fireman? A doctor? A nurse? A teacher?

What is a teacher? (*Someone who teaches*) What is a teacher doing when he or she teaches? A teacher helps someone to learn. In preschool and school there are lots of teachers. They help children learn to read and write and work with numbers. Your parents are also your teachers. What has Mom or Dad shown you how to do? (*brush your teeth, put on your clothes, tie your shoe laces, ride a bike, etc.*)

Do you know that you don't have to be a grownup to be a teacher? *You* are teachers already! Have you ever helped your sister or brother get dressed or put toys away? Guess what! You are being a teacher when you do that. Or maybe you showed your grandfather or grandmother how to use a computer! Yes, that's teaching, too.

You also teach us grownups when you help us to worship, especially when you sing for us. Do you know what you teach us? You teach us to praise God and to make a joyful noise to the Lord. For some of us, it seems strange to clap, or to raise our hands and say "Hallelujah" or "Praise the Lord." You show us not to be shy to do that, and we have fun doing it with you. Sometimes we grownups have so many other things on our minds that we forget that Jesus gives us joy. You remind us that knowing Jesus makes us happy. When you sing songs like *"Swing Low, Sweet Chariot" and "When the Saints Go Marchin' In," it helps us to think about how wonderful and marvelous it will be when we all get to heaven. (*Substitute appropriate songs known to the children.)

When you are showing others what to do—teaching them—you are also being like Jesus. Jesus was a teacher. He told the people who followed him, (*Read from Mark 10:14,15*) "Let the little children come to me; do not stop them; for it is to such as these that the kingdom of heaven belongs. Truly I tell you, whoever does not receive the kingdom of God as a little child will never enter it." Jesus said that the kingdom of heaven belongs to people who are like you children. For many of us here today, it's been a long time since we were children. But we need to trust and believe in Jesus the same way you do. And all of us who believe in Jesus are God's children. It doesn't matter if we are big or small. God adopted us and all of us call God our Father.

There are other ways and times and places where you can be teachers, too. When you are being loving and kind, or giving and sharing, you are showing other people how to be like Jesus. Whether you are in church, at home, at daycare, at school, on the playground, or shopping with Mom or Dad, you can teach your playmates, your classmates, and strangers how Jesus wants us to be like him.

Stretching Further:

Have the children sing a favorite song of theirs with motions. Let the congregation learn the motions and sing along.

So, thank you, children, for showing us and teaching us how to be joyful. To help you to remember to go on being teachers about God, I have a card for each of you. (*Show a card.*) It says, **My name is** _____. On the line you can write your name, or ask Dad or Mom to write it for you. It also says, **I am a teacher.** This week your parents can help you to write on the card the things you have done to show and teach others how to be like Jesus. When you bring the cards back next week, we can share them with one another if you like. I don't have enough cards to give to all the people here, but you have helped us grownups to remember, too, that what we do and say shows what we believe and who(m) we believe.

Before I give you your card, let's pray. Please bow your heads and repeat after me:

Dear God, thank you for sending Jesus to teach us about you. Help us to be like him in all we say and do. Let us be good teachers, too. We pray in Jesus' name. Amen.

Talking To God

Theme: Anyone can talk to God anytime, anywhere, in any way.

Scripture: The Lord hears when I call to him.—Psalm 4:3b

Preparation: On 3" x 12" poster board cards, print with a broad black marker one of these words per card: anybody, anyone, any way, anyhow, anyplace, anywhere, anytime, anything.

Have you ever helped a grownup to do some work? Maybe you have helped to make cookies, clean your room, dry dishes, or dust furniture. Or have you planted seeds, pulled weeds, picked berries, or watered flowers? Has anyone helped to wash the car?

A boy named Alex was helping his grandfather rake leaves one day. His grandfather heard him say, "God, this is hard work!"

"Alex, what did you say?" his grandfather asked.

Alex said, "I wasn't talking to you, Grandpa."

To whom do you think Alex was talking? Alex was talking to God. Sometimes that's what we say praying is — talking to God.

When should we talk to God? Are there special times when you say prayers at home? (*At bedtime, before meals, etc.*) From the Bible we know that special times of prayer for the Jewish people were at nine o'clock in the morning, at noon, at three o'clock in the afternoon and at sunset in the evening. But the Apostle Paul wrote,

"Pray in the Spirit at all times. . . . " (Ephesians 6:18a) And Paul wrote, "Pray without ceasing." (I Thessalonians 5:17) That means we should never stop praying. We can pray anytime and all the time.

I like to talk to God when I'm doing something that doesn't need my mind to do much thinking, like standing in line at the grocery store or sitting in a doctor's waiting room. I pray when I'm swimming or driving on a road I've driven many times before.

Could you talk to God when you're riding a bus or walking to or from school? What other times could you pray? When you are sad, afraid, alone, angry or upset, when you need to forgive someone or be forgiven—those are all times when it's good to pray. Good times to pray are also when you are happy, when you want to thank God for something or ask God to bless someone.

Where should we pray? Often we pray together in church, where people see us praying. Jesus said (*Read from Bible Matthew 6:5*), "But whenever you pray, go into your room and shut the door and pray to your Father who is in secret; and your Father who sees in secret will reward you." We should pray when we're alone, too, where no one sees us praying. Have you ever been sent to your room for "time out" because you've done something wrong? That would be a good time and place to pray, wouldn't it?

Jesus went many times to a mountain where he could be alone to pray. And when he was dying on the cross, the last thing he did was to talk to God.

I hope you know, as Alex does, that you can talk to God anytime and anywhere, and God listens. Whether we talk out loud, whisper, or just think our prayers, God hears. In the book of Psalms David wrote, "The Lord hears when I call to him." (Psalm 4:3b) Jesus said, "Your Father knows what you need before you ask him" (Matthew 6:8b). God knows what we wish for and what we're afraid of. And when we have hard work to do, God is ready to help us do it.

Here are some important words to remember about talking to God. (*Show word cards, in order, one at a time, while saying, "God loves us and cares for us so much that anyone and anybody can pray and talk to God in* any way, anyhow, anyplace, anywhere *at* anytime *and ask for* anything." Can you say these words with me? (*Repeat.*)

Let's pray now. Today let each of us talk to God quietly and know that God is listening. Please close your eyes and bow your heads. (*Allow a minute or two.*) We pray in Jesus' name. Amen.

Stretching Further:

Ask children to share their favorite mealtime or bedtime prayers. How many of them use the same prayer? Would they like to learn a new prayer?

~

Be Wise

Theme: Wisdom comes from God.

Scripture: But if any of you needs wisdom, you should ask God for it. God is generous. He enjoys giving to all people, so God will give you wisdom.—James 1:5

Preparation: 1. Read I Kings 3:4–14. 2. Print the following passages from the *International Children's Bible* on separate 4" x 6" index cards:

A. Happiness makes a person smile.—Proverbs 15:13

B. Don't ever stop being kind and truthful.—Proverbs 3:3a

C. Don't ever say things that are not true.—Proverbs 4:24b

D. Trust the Lord with all your heart.—Proverbs 3:5a

E. Wisdom will help you be a good person. It will help you do what is right. —Proverbs 2:20

3. As the children gather, give one card to each of five older children who are able to read them.

If someone told you that you could have anything you wanted, what would you ask for?

This happened to a young man named Solomon. When his father, King David, died, Solomon became the king of his people. But Solomon wasn't sure that he knew how to be a good king.

Then God came to Solomon in a dream and said, "Ask for anything you want, and I will give it to you." (I Kings 3:5)

Do you know what Solomon asked for? He asked for wisdom. Do you know what wisdom is? Wisdom is good sense, knowing how to find the answer to a problem, using what you know to help yourself or others. Solomon asked for wisdom so that he could rule the people in the right way. He needed wisdom to know the difference between right and wrong, good and bad.

Do you think God gave Solomon what he asked for? Yes. God keeps promises. God gave Solomon wisdom and understanding. And God also gave him things he didn't ask for. God gave him riches and honor. And God promised that Solomon would live a long life if he obeyed God's rules.

So Solomon was a wise king. As he grew older, he wrote down some of what he had learned. We can read what he wrote in the book called Proverbs: Wise Teachings for God's People. (*Show Bible, opened to Proverbs.*) Let's hear a few of Solomon's wise teachings. (*Call on the children to read the index cards aloud, one at a time. After each reading, ask if the children agree that it is a true, good, wise teaching to follow today.*)

It is good to be wise, to have wisdom. So how do we get wisdom? How did Solomon get wisdom? He asked God for it.

In the book called James, he wrote, (*Read from Bible James 1:5*) . . . "if any of you needs wisdom, you should ask God for it. God is generous. He enjoys giving to all people, so God will give you wisdom." When you need to know what is the best thing to do, or what is good and what is bad, pray and ask God to tell you what to do. And after you ask, then listen for God's answer. Sometimes God's answer will be to talk with your parents. They might help you to find what you need to know in the Bible. You may not be a king or a queen, a president, a preacher or a teacher, but God enjoys giving to all people, even to you and me. And God enjoys giving gifts to us every day.

Let's pray now:

All-wise God, we thank you for the wisdom that you gave to Solomon long ago. Thank you that we can ask you for whatever we need. We are glad that you like to give. Help us to use the gifts you give us to help others to know you. Amen.

Stretching Further: Play an improvised game of Solomon Says, fashioned after the traditional Simon Says. (*See page 44 "Jesus Says."*) If the saying follows Solomon's wisdom, the children respond by saying, "Wise!" If the saying is not something Solomon would teach, the children say, "Not wise!" (or "Unwise!")

～

God Forgets

Theme: God forgives and forgets the wrong things we've done.

Scripture: For I will be merciful toward their iniquities, and I will remember their sins no more.—Hebrews 8:12

Preparation: Bookmark Hebrews 8:12.

I have a problem. Sometimes I forget things. *This morning I got into my car to drive to church. Then I had to go back inside my house because I forgot my car keys. Once I went to the swimming pool, but I couldn't go into the water. What do you think I forgot? My swimsuit! And another time I wanted to stop at the grocery store on my way home, but I forgot! I had to turn around and go back or we wouldn't have had any milk for breakfast.

Have you ever forgotten something very important? (*a book, your lunch or lunch money, homework, your glasses, a permission slip, a musical instrument?*) Have you ever forgotten to do something that's important? (*to feed your pet, make your bed, a special job at home, schoolwork?*)

When we forget things, we say that we are forgetful. Do you think God is forgetful? Why?/Why not? I think there are things that God doesn't remember. Listen to what God said (*Read from the Bible Hebrews 8:12.*), "For I will be merciful toward their iniquities, and I will remember their sins no more." Iniquities is another word for sins. Sins are things we do that are wrong, things that are against God's law. Can you think of wrong things that boys and girls sometimes do? (*making fun of someone, saying unkind things to or about someone, teasing or bullying another child, taking something that doesn't belong to them, fighting, talking back or yelling at their parents, not doing what they are told to do, not sharing toys, cheating in a game or on tests, copying someone else's homework, etc.*) God wants us to be kind, to love one another, and to obey our parents.

What can you do when you know **you** have done something wrong? You can say "I was wrong," "I'm sorry," and "forgive me" to the person you have hurt. You can give back something that you've taken that isn't yours. If you haven't done what you were asked to do, do it. And you can ask God to forgive you and help you to do better. When you are sorry for what you've done and you ask God for forgiveness, God will forgive and forget that you ever did those bad things. We deserve to be punished for our sins, and sometimes we are. Even though God loves us, God doesn't like the wrong things we do. But God doesn't keep a record of them. God chooses to forget; God will "remember them no more."

I imagine that when God says he will not remember my sins, it is something like what happens on a rainy day. Have you ever watched a car's windshield wipers going back and forth, wiping away raindrops? (*Demonstrate with your hands.*) Those wipers make me think of God wiping my sins away. Move your hands back and forth with me. Think about God wiping away all the wrong things we've done. When God forgives us, God makes us feel good and clean, like we've just had a bath or shower that washed our sins away.

Let's pray now. Please bow your heads and repeat after me. (*Say short, meaningful phrases.*)

Forgive me, God, for things I've done that are not kind and good. Forgive me, and help me try to do the things I should. In Jesus' name I pray. Amen.

Stretching Further:

Has anyone ever done anything to make you angry or sad? What can you do? You can talk about it with your parents or teachers. In Paul's letter to the people called Ephesians he wrote, "Be kind to one another, tenderhearted, forgiving one another, as God in Christ has forgiven you" (Ephesians 4:32). You can be like a windshield wiper, too, (*use hand motions*) and forgive that person. And like God, you can choose to forget. Then try to help him or her to do better.

∼

Three-in-one

Theme: Our God is three persons and at the same time one.

Scripture: Now when all the people were baptized, and when Jesus also had been baptized and was praying, the heaven was opened, and the Holy Spirit descended upon him in bodily form like a dove. And a voice came from heaven, "You are my Son, the Beloved; with you I am well pleased."—Luke 3:21–22

Preparation: Draw or obtain a large picture of a leaf of a shamrock (a clover with three leaflets). Bookmark Luke 3:21–22.

Who likes to do things with numbers? Who likes to count? Have you learned to add numbers? Subtract? Multiply? Divide? Does anyone like to do puzzles with numbers?

I'm going to ask you some questions about numbers in the Bible. Let's see what you have learned. (*Note: all answers are "three."*) How many gifts did the wise men give to Jesus? (*three: gold, frankincense, myrrh*) When Jesus hung on the cross, how many crosses were on that hill? How many times did Peter say that he didn't know Jesus? How long was Jesus in the tomb before he rose again? (*parts of three days*) It seems that things often happened in threes.

Three is a very important number in the Bible. In fact, we say that God is *three* persons who are at the same time *one*. Our God is God the Father, God the Son (Jesus Christ), and God the Holy Spirit. And yet our God is *one* God. *One* is also a very important number in the Bible.

It's not easy for us to understand this mystery: how God can be three persons and at the same time our one and only God. Saint Patrick used a shamrock to tell the people of Ireland about God. (*Show picture.*) The leaf of a shamrock, which we call a clover, has three leaflets. Each little part, each leaflet, is a part of the same clover. Without the three parts, it would not be a shamrock.

In the Bible we see the three persons of God working together, while each one does a separate task. Listen to hear what each one does. (*Read Luke 3:21–22.*) What did Jesus—God the Son—do? (*Jesus was baptized; Jesus prayed.*) What did God the Holy Spirit do? (*The Holy Spirit came down on Jesus in the form of a dove, a bird.*) What did God the Father do? (*God the Father said to Jesus, "You are my Son. I love you. I'm very pleased with you."* [paraphrased]) And when **we** are baptized, we are baptized in the name of the Father, and of the Son, and of the Holy Spirit.

Remember that God, our heavenly Father, is the person to whom we pray, the one who watches over us. Jesus, God the Son, is the person who came to earth to show us what God the Father is like. Jesus died so that we can join God's family. The Holy Spirit is the person who helps us to learn and grow as God's children.

Our God is an awesome God, greater than we can imagine or understand or explain.

This awesome three-in-one God created the world and all that is in it. How wonderful that God goes on working, taking care of us, and loving us. And God invites each of us to join in this work by caring for one another and for all that God has created.

Let's pray. Please bow your heads and repeat after me. (Say *short meaningful phrases.*)

Dear God, we do not understand how you can be three persons in one. But we do know this—that you love us, and watch over us, and teach us. Thank you, God. You are awesome. We pray in the name of Jesus. Amen.

Stretching Further: Talk about the word *Trinity*, a word not found in the Bible. We use *Trinity* to mean that we believe that God is three-in-one: the Father, the Son, and the Holy Spirit. Another word we use to tell about God being three-in-one is *Triune*. *Trinity* and *Triune* both begin with "t-r-i," which means three. What other words do you know that begin with "t-r-i"? (*tricycle, trio, triangle, triceratops [a dinosaur with three horns], triple, triplet, etc.*)

∽

Be Salty

Theme: You can flavor your world with love.

Scripture: You are the salt of the earth.—Matthew 5:13a

Preparation: Gather an assortment of salt shakers of different sizes, shapes and colors.

I've brought some things to show you. (*Show several salt shakers.*) Do you know what they are? These are salt shakers. (*Show remaining shakers, pointing out different sizes, shapes and colors.*)

Why do we use salt shakers? What kinds of food do you like with salt on it? Does the salt make those foods taste better?

Do you know that salt is used in many other ways? If we sprinkle salt on ice, the ice melts. But salt also helps ice cream to freeze. At one time, people used salt to keep food from spoiling. Without food, they couldn't live, so salt became very valuable. Salt was so valuable that Roman soldiers long ago were paid with salt instead of money. In some places salt was worth as much as gold.

Can we find anything in the Bible about salt? In Matthew 5:13, Jesus said, "You are the salt of the earth." And in Mark 9:50, he said, "Have salt in yourselves, and be at peace with one another."

How can **we** be the salt of the earth? Just as salt brings out the best flavor in food, we can help to bring out the best in other people. We can try not to quarrel or fight. When we do good, kind things, we are being "salty," as Jesus wants us to be. We can salt the earth by showing our love and by telling everyone that God loves them.

How do you feel when you eat a lot of salty food? Thirsty? When people see how you are showing love, you can make them thirsty to know more about Jesus.

We are like these salt shakers. Each one of us is different. By living the way Jesus showed us— loving one another— **we** can be "salt shakers."

Let's pray: **Dear God, thank you for salt to make our food taste better. We want to be salty for you. Help us to sprinkle everything we do with love, in Jesus' name. Amen.**

The next time you eat pretzels, popcorn, corn on the cob, or French fries with salt, remember that **you** are the salt of the earth, and salt is very valuable and important.

Stretching Further: Talk about the use of salt to show friendship and hospitality. Giving salt as a present to friends in their new home is a custom in some countries. In Russia, salt and bread are used in ceremonies to welcome guests. Bread is a symbol of a wish that the guests may never be hungry; and the salt, that their lives will always be full of flavor.

⌒

Saying Thank You

Theme: Being thankful

Scripture: It is good to give thanks to the Lord.—Psalm 92:1a

Preparation: 1. Print with marker on two separate large cards **thank** and **you**.

2. On index cards (one per child), print **My name is** _____. **God loves me. Thank you, God.**

Today I'm thinking about two little words. The first word is (*Show cards*) **thank.** And the second word is **you.** When do you say thank you? (*Allow time for children to respond to questions.*) Who do you say thank you to? Have you already said thank you to someone today? Why?

Have you ever done anything that made someone say thank you to you? Can you tell us about what you did?

After someone says thank you, what do you say? I hope you say "You're welcome" or "I'm happy I could do that," or "I'm glad I could give you that."

We've talked about people you thank. (*Show word cards* **you** and **thank**) The Bible tells us (*Read Psalm 92:10*) "It is good to give thanks to the Lord." Let's all say that verse together. (*Repeat the verse with the children.*) Another name for the Lord is God.

So we should also say thank you to God. What has God given us? (*Jesus, love, happiness, food, families, friends, teachers, a place to live, clothing, rain, sunshine, etc.*) We read in Ephesians 5:20 (*Read from Bible*) "Always give thanks to God the Father for **everything** in the name of our Lord Jesus Christ."

Saying thank you and you're welcome is a way of showing love to someone. Do you know that all of the people here today love you? Let's shout "Thank you for loving me" to them. Then we'll listen (*Put your hand behind your ear*) to hear what they say to us. Ready? (*Say with the children*) **Thank you for loving me.** (*After congregation responds, clap your hands.*)

There's one very special person we haven't named, one that you should be thankful for. That's **you**. You should be thankful to God for **you**. You are a miracle. David wrote to God in a Psalm (139:14), "I praise you because you made me in an amazing and wonderful way." And there is no one else exactly like you, even if you are an identical twin. Don't forget to thank God for **you**.

Stretching Further:

Hand out index cards. Tell children to write their name, or to ask their parents to write the child's name on the card. Then put it in your Bible, on your dresser, on a bulletin board, on your wall or door. It will remind you every day to thank God for loving you.

Let's pray: **Dear God, in the name of Jesus, thank you for everything. Thank you for making me and for loving me. Help me to show my love every day by thanking you and by thanking others. Amen.**

$\sim$

Bibliography

ABC's of the Bible: Intriguing Questions and Answers about the Greatest Book Ever Written. Pleasantville, N.Y.: Reader's Digest Association, 1991.

Dallas Seminary Faculty. *The Bible Knowledge Commentary: An Exposition of the Scriptures*. Ed. John F. Walvoord and Roy B. Zuck. Wheaton, Ill.: Victor Books, 1985.

Eliasson, Kelsey. *Polar Bears of Churchill*. Churchill, Manitoba: Munck's Café, 2006.

Good News for Modern Man: The New Testament in Today's English Version. New York: American Bible Society, 1966.

Holy Bible: International Children's Bible, New Century Version. Dallas, Texas: Word Publishing, 1988.

Holy Bible: New Revised Standard Version Bible. National Council of the Churches of Christ in the United States of America. Grand Rapids, Mich.: Zondervan, 1989.

Life Application Bible: New International Version. Wheaton, Ill.: Thyndale House, and Grand Rapids, Mich.: Zondervan, 1991.

Miller, Madeleine S. and J. Lane Miller. *The New Harper's Bible Dictionary*. New York: Harper & Row, 1973.

The Promise:Contemporary English Version. Nashville, Tenn: Thomas Nelson, 1995.

Sing-a-long Songbook 3, "God's Not Dead." Mobile, Ala.: Integrity Music, 1993.

United Methodist Hymnal. Nashville, Tenn.: United Methodist Publishing House, 1989.

Index